3 SIMPLE STEPS

For Your Marketing Your Local Business Online

How To Use Video & Social Media Marketing To Dominate Your Competition

BILLY STICKER

Table of Contents

How to Use The Internet to Slash Your Advertising Budget... (47)

chapter 1 | Introduction

There's no doubt that social media has become a game changer in the marketing and branding of your business online. The past 10 to 15 years was a totally different set of projects for you to launch in an online marketing campaign compared to what it is today, and most of that has to do with social media.

There was a book that came out 10 to 15 years ago by a professor named Robert Cialdini. The book is called *Influence: The Psychology of Persuasion.* It became an instant classic. What Dr. Cialdini did in his book was break down six triggers that affect human behavior, that affect why we make the decisions we do, and just our overall psychology of persuasion.

It helps you get into the mind of your client and understand why and how it is they make the decisions that they do, which can be extremely profitable and beneficial to you as you set forth any marketing campaign or just any kind of business in general, understanding why people make the decisions they do. So the book is, hands down, one of the best business books of the past

10 to 15 years and one that I would highly recommend you pick up from your library if you've not read it yet.

But what I want to do right now is take a look at the six triggers that Dr. Cialdini wrote about in his book, and let's apply them to social media and see how they intertwine and overlap today.

1. Reciprocity:

The first one that he identified is reciprocity, which reciprocity is simply people pay in kind. If you ever go to a department store or go to the mall and there's two sets of double doors, if you hold the first set of double doors open for someone walking up behind you, they almost always will hold the second set of doors open for you. Psychologically inside of us, we almost feel we have to do that to repay somebody who just did the same for us.

And the reason that's beneficial in marketing, especially later on in the book when we get into content and how to actually reach your clients, the more and more that you can give, the more they feel obligated to give back to you. So reciprocity, people repay in kind. You give them a little bit, they feel like they need to give you a little bit back.

2. Social Proof:

The second trigger is social proof. People follow the lead of others who are similar. And obviously in social media, most of their connections and contact, whether it's on Facebook or Google+ or Twitter, depending on where your clients are at—and that's something we'll get into later in the book, finding out where you even need to get started in social media—but they tend to follow people like them and people that they look up to. Well, social proof basically just says that they're going to make some of the decisions they do, almost back to peer pressure in high school, wearing the same type of clothes, the same brands.

People want to be accepted, and they want to know that all of these other people are making the same type of decisions. They know if they make the same type of decisions that they will be accepted with this other group they tend to be following online. And it's very subconscious that we do that, but it is a trigger that happens to us daily, and you see it advertised and used in marketing in different types of media thousands of times a day, just social proof. The more celebrities you see drinking a certain drink or wearing a certain type of clothes the more people want to go out and drink those same drinks and wear those same clothes.

3. Liking:

Number three is liking. And this just has to do with relationships. People tend not to follow people on Facebook that they just don't like. Now there are some people that will, but for the most part, you want to be around people you like, and you want to do business with people you trust.

Years ago my wife and I were out looking to buy our first vehicle—this has been almost 17 years ago—and we had such a hard time finding a decent salesperson in a car lot. It was amazing the types of people we would deal with. Well, there was one salesperson in particular that we really did have a liking to, and when it came down to finally making the decision to buy the vehicle, we decided we were going to look at the same vehicle at her lot, and then we were taking those numbers down the street and going to another one.

And she had brought up the comment that we had spent a lot of time together and we had a really good relationship, that there was some trust the salesperson felt she had built with us, and we agreed. And that was the close that she used on us, basically, is,"We have a relationship.Please go talk to the other company first, then come back here." Would 400 or $500 even make that much of a difference to us? But that taught us this exact principle: liking.

We decided at that moment, even if it was 400 or $500 more to get the new vehicle through her, we were going to go through her because people like to do business with people they like, even if it means spending a little more money sometimes. Because there's a lot of people whom I refuse to do business with if I don't like them. So that has to do with the third thing, which was liking.

4. Authority:

Number four is authority. People defer to experts. Online and in social media, you need to become the expert in your field, and you do not have to wait for permission. There's a statement that says, "Fake it until you make it." If you know more about a given subject matter than the majority of your audience, that makes you the expert. You go read five books on a certain topic that most people don't know that much about, you are now an expert over the majority of people on that topic.

So online, when it comes to social media, when someone appears to come across as an expert, that gives them more credibility, more influence, and more persuasion. So do your best to position yourself and your company, your product, your service, as the authority in your industry.

5. Scarcity:

Scarcity is basically a way to create urgency. People psychologically and subconsciously want more of what they can't have. And if they feel there is a shortage or there's a limited-time offer and they must act now, it creates this urgency inside them that affects their ability to make decisions.They want to make that decision quicker because of this desire not to miss out,especially when you tie in these other key ingredients: the social proof, the reciprocity, the authority, the liking.

When you tie all these together, and there's a sense of urgency that's there, it makes people want to make a decision faster. So that's another way that the social media ties in with the psychology of persuasion.

6. Commitments and Consistency:

And then the sixth thing is commitment and consistency. The more commitment and consistency that people see online, over time, the same message, the same values, the same authority, the same expertise, the same liking, that builds trust, which ties back into liking and a lot of the other things. So when they say commitment and consistency, that's another huge psychological trigger when it comes to persuasion.

So during your social media campaign, remember to build trust through consistency and commitment in whatever it is you're doing. Social media builds on each of these triggers. To help us understand why our clients make the decisions they do, as we go on through the rest of the book, keep these six triggers in mind:

→ Reciprocity: People want to give back when someone gives to them.

→ Social proof: Peer pressure. People feel accepted doing what others are doing too.

→ Liking: We want to be around people we like and are similar to us.

→ Authority: We have a built-in desire to follow the expert. Be the expert.

→ Scarcity: Desire to have things that are rare or fear of missing out. Urgency.

→ Commitment and Consistency: Builds trust. Not all change is good. Stability, security.

We will keep these in the forefront of our minds as we go through the rest of the book, building your social media marketing campaign.

chapter 2 | Step 1 – Purpose

Biggest Online Marketing Myth:

The biggest myth of online marketing is that your website is the most important thing online.

That is a myth, and we will get more into that later. Marketing your business online is not focused around your website. With the exception, if you make actual sales and transactions from your website. But the majority of local businesses have a website or web presence that's just meant to get their local phone to ring and to drive traffic into their local business. We'll focus more on that in a second.

Purpose of Business:

First, let's look at what your purpose is for your business in general. The purpose of any business is to make profit.

What you need to do is define where you are in your business and what your exact goals are for your profit. In other words, are you at the time of your life where right now your goal is to grow your business for a lifestyle because you need more money, because you want to create a legacy in your business that you can pass down to generations? Or maybe you want to build your business to get ready to sell your business to a different company and retire?

→ Grow your business?

→ Sell it?

→ Leave it to family?

→ Hire more?

→ Lifestyle?

→ Etc.

Those are decisions that you have to make, but that would definitely carry weight and should have great input on how you market your company into the future.

So our first goal is to determine exactly what your personal goals are for your business and the profits that you bring in.

Today's Economy

In today's economy clients and customers are more frugal than they ever have been before. They are more educated, mostly because of the Internet.

→ They get online and read reviews of your company, your product.

→ They can watch reviews on YouTube.

→ They check the Better Business Bureau.

→ They can even get on Amazon and look at reviews of products that maybe you sell that are sold on there also.

Customers today study before they make decisions. Because of that, you need to do everything you can do to position yourself—just like we talked about in the earlier chapter on the psychology of persuasion—position yourself as an expert in your authority.

Traditional advertising is broken.

If you look at traditional advertising over the past 20 to 30 years, and even shorter, look at what's happened in television. Now we have DVR and Internet TV. What this has done is greatly reduce the effectiveness of television advertising. People either fast forward through the commercials or they don't even use their television; they get on the Internet and watch their programming on demand without having to watch any unnecessary advertisements.

Traditional	New Technlogy
TV	DVR, DVD, Internet
Radio	Satellite Radio, Pandora, Internet, smart phones
Newspaper	Circulation Down Internet
Magazine	" " "
Phonebook	Smart phones, Search engines

"The good news is, your competition is faced with the same problem."

On the radio today there's a huge growth in satellite radio and Internet radio. And with smartphones growing also and unlimited Internet available on their phones, people can now create their own radio stations without having to listen to any radio advertising.

Look at newspapers, magazines. Circulations of these traditional publications are at an all-time low. Even though there are some on the computer, it's still not nearly as effective as what it has been in the past.

Yellow Pages, an extremely expensive marketing route has become more and more ineffective. Ninety-seven percent of the people interviewed said they throw their

Yellow Pages—their phonebooks—away when they receive them.

With smartphones, people basically have access to the entire Internet in the palm of their hands virtually at all times. So when they need to look up a phone number, a business, a product, or a service, it's readily available to them, which in turn, makes phonebook advertising obsolete.

Each sale or transaction that you make has never been more important.

In the same aspect, each transaction or sale that you *lose* has never been more important.

Most people think if they lose a sale to a competition, it just costs them that one sale. That's not the case.

Let's look at how one lost sale to the competition will cost you five times what you think it would. How is that really the cost?

Each Lost Sale Costs You 5 Lost Sales!

1. **You lose that transaction.** Any profit that was made on that transaction is now gone, and the majority of that goes just because you received

or someone received a brand new customer, a brand new contact.

2. **Any chance of an upsell to make more profit** on that same transaction or bumping them to a different product.

3. **You lose any repeat business.** If your competition is doing a good job building relationships, then their new client has no reason to go anywhere else.

4. **Any referrals that this new client gets** will be going to the new business that they chose.

5. **Your competition now has that extra money to go out and put back into advertising to take more and more of your customers away**.

It's very important that you understand every transaction is five times more valuable than what you think it is.

And five times more valuable, that's over 100% return on investment for each transaction that you can win.

Your Advantage Over Your Competition:

Now, you have a great advantage because your competition still believes the myth we spoke about at the beginning of this chapter, that their website is one of the most important things to market online. Well, we know that's not the case. We know more. And because *you have this book*, we will breakdown all of the different ways where we can outmaneuver and outsmart your competition.

Our purpose is to use social media and other sites to dominate your online presence, not for people to go to your website, but for people to call your phone, knock on your door, and hand you money.

Use this book to dominate your competition. That way each sale you take from them cost them 5sales!

chapter 3 | # Step 2 - Planning

The Only 3 Ways to Grow a Business

There are only three ways to grow the bottom-line profit of any business.

1. New customers or clients

2. Larger transactions

3. More frequent transactions

Most companies focus on only getting new customers. If you increased only 10% in each one of these areas, 10% new customers, 10% larger transactions, and 10% more frequent transactions, you did not just grow your business by 10%. You grew your business by over 30% as far as company profits go.

So as we look into marketing your business online, keep in mind that our planning is not just toward new customers; it's towards increasing each one of these three areas as we can: 1)new customers and clients, 2) larger transactions, and 3)more frequent transactions.

If we can grow each one of those areas, it will drastically multiply your return on your investment for any marketing that you do.

Identify your perfect prospect.

Do you have a database for your business already? I strongly recommend that you do,whether it's to capture simply names and emails to put on a list, or it's a database that has customers' address, phone numbers, anything that you can use to reach back out. Your money is in your customer list.

Knowing your database.

Online some people refer to this as an avatar, and the idea behind it is to actually design your perfect customer and have that person in mind. Know them.

→ Who are they?

→ Male, female?

→ What are their occupations,

→ their recreations,

→ their motivations?

→ What makes them happy?

→ What keeps them awake at night?

→ What are their top three biggest problems that they deal with?

→ Or maybe it's their values in certain areas that you relate to with your business.

You have to know who your ideal, perfect customer is, and your marketing needs to be designed towards that ideal demographic.

The more you know, the more effectively you can communicate and connect with that market and the more trust that that builds.

Internet marketing isn't about turning everyone online into a prospect. Our goal is to identify your ideal, most profitable prospect and bring as many of those people to you as possible and keep them coming back and referring their friends and doing more and more business with you. That is our goal.

The 5 C's of Social Marketing

1. **Crowd:** which represents everyone. You must know that everyone online is not a prospect. Know exactly who your customer is. Those are the people that we're looking for online.

2. **Community**. This is your ideal prospect or influencers in that demographic: your customers, referrals, et cetera.

   When identified, it's easier to locate where these prospects go online. What Facebooks groups? Are they on Twitter? Are they on forums? Are they on Google+? When you know exactly who your target demographic is, it's easier for us to go and find them to be able to market to them.

3. **Concerns**. This is where research comes in, and it goes back to knowing your demographic. Your community typically gets online, and when they go to a search engine, they're trying to do research to solve a problem. They have a concern; you should hopefully have that solution.

   When they look for a problem, we want you to be the ones that they find with the solution—the trust agent. They search for answers; they get the research; and we want that research to hopefully be provided by you as far as the content, which brings us into the fourth C.

4. **Content** Their research leads to your content. Your content is the solution to their problems, the answers to what keeps them up at night.

The money they have to spend on solving their problems, hopefully they find what they need in your content,which will trigger Reciprocity, and they will want to do business with you.

When they read your content, whether the content is an article, a blog post, an email, a video, an audio that they listen to, when that content is there and it answers their question and is their solution, it positions you as the expert and the authority,which goes back to building trust and ties into the six key elements we talked earlier about in the psychology of persuasion.

So now, with your content building you as an expert, we hope to funnel those C's down into the fifth C, which are customers or clients. These are the ones who found your content and realized it solved problems.

They now trust and they call you and choose to do business with you. The three most important words in sales are relationship, relationship, relationship, just like they say the three most important words in real estate are location, location, location.

Our job online is to position you as the expert and to develop as much content as possible that positions you as the expert that helps them build trust with you. When it's time for them to decide to make the decision of where to do business, you are automatically who they're going to call because of the Psychology of Influence that we discussed earlier.

*Note, invest in quality people skills, customer service training. Your employees must understand all of these same principles, also. So take the time to not only learn this yourself, but teach this to some of your key employees that they can teach others so everyone is on the same page.

chapter 4 | Step 3 – Presence

The saying goes, "content is king." Whether it's Google, Bing, Yahoo, or any other search engine, these companies know people search online for answers. Earlier we discussed the myth that marketing online is to drive website traffic. This is only true if you sell directly from your website. Our goal is for you to be found throughout your content. Your content simply answers to your community's concerns, which we talked about in the five C's.

Smartphones multiply the importance of you having great content available online. There are different types of content. There can be articles, which may be a blog post, an ezine article, sometimes referred to as white papers or PDFs, ebooks. There could be video presentations, webinars, Power Point, or slide show presentations that have been recorded. Some of the content could also just be audio, a podcast, a teleseminar, interviews with other leading experts in your industry.

Content can be a variety of these types of things, and it's great to offer as many of these as possible because the more content that's available online, the more arrows will be pointing back to your phone number and to your front door.

Mike Koenigs of Traffic Geyser has a great formula for developing content for videos. He calls it his 10x10x4 formula. We're just going to look at a portion of that. He says a great way to come up with content is to take the top 10 frequently asked questions about your company, product, or service, turn each one of those top 10 questions into content by answering the content. That could be 10 different articles, 10 different blog posts, 10 videos, 10 audios. There's 30 different types of content just right there that you could do.

Then, you should also not have the top 10 frequently asked questions, but you should also have the top 10 questions that people should be asking about your company, service, or product,and do the same thing with these 10. You could have articles, videos, audios. You could have them transcribed. And there's another 30 or more pieces of content just right there.

And his last four mini videos he talks about in his—you know, the 10x10x4 formula, are about buying stuff and more information and things like that. So we're not going to get into that.

But your presence online will greatly be determined by the amount and quality of content that you have. The important content is going to be key. And you want to have keyword-specific content in your titles and throughout your message. I encourage you to go to Google and search 'keyword tools'. Play around with different types of keywords in your industry that have to do with the content you would need to develop. Remember, this content is answering questions and helping solve problems for your customers.

Some people are afraid to solve these answers and solve these problems because they feel that if they solve these problems for their customers in the content, why would the customers want to come do business with them if they've just solved the problem with the content. This goes back to Reciprocity. If you're giving away good, quality information and the prospect or your client trusts you because of that, and they feel if the free information you give away is of such high quality, when it's time to do business, they're going to be that much more likely to do business with you because you gave them something of value. You're an expert. They trust you. There's social proof. It all ties back to those six fundamental areas we talked about at the very beginning of the book.

So your content should be relevant, should be filled with keywords, which will help you be found online through these search engines. It needs to be relevant; it needs to be a great value. You can have a call-to-action in these videos and articles. A call-to-action would simply be, for more information or if you have more questions about this topic or need help, call this number, come to this address, email us, whatever call-to-action you want the next step for that client to be. But it's very important that there is always a call-to-action at the end of your content.

Also, have all of your contact information, whether it's in the video description, the bottom of the blog post. You need to have your website, your phone number, email, your physical address, your Facebook page, your Twitter page, your YouTube channel, any of the social media platforms that you are currently using. You need to have all of those in your contact information for people to be able to get in touch with you.

Set up accounts with all of the social media sites that have to do with content sharing. These are video-sharing sites, article directories, podcast directories, and et cetera. What this does is allow us to take your content, distribute it using certain tools amongst all of these hundreds and hundreds of websites out there, and all of this content is targeted with your keywords, and it all points back to you, your phone number, your company, your address, your place of business.

I want to end this chapter with three other ideas for content. One is you can outsource content. You can find people online who will actually write and create your content for you. That's one of the services that our company provides. Some of your content could be testimonials, which I highly encourage you to do. When you have good reviews from your clients, ask them to record a short video or to write something down or simply pose for a picture and have you write something down that you can post online, then you can use a collection of these testimonials to make videos. All this does is go back to building social proof and acceptance.

Google also offers a great tool called Google Alerts. Simply go to Google and type in 'alerts'. It will allow you to set up alerts for certain keywords targeting your industry. You can even set your company's name in there. And what will happen is any time you are mentioned or that keyword is mentioned online, whether it's in newsfeeds, in blog posts, or whatever it may be, Google will send you an email and a text message with the links to those websites. So Google Alerts is a great way for you to stay on top of and develop even more content for your social media campaign.

chapter 5 | Putting it into Practice

Now that we have covered the Purpose, Plan, & Presence, let's look at some practical applications. It's far too easy to gather information compared to applying it.

It's the difference of knowledge and wisdom.

→ Knowledge is education, information, the "How to…"

→ Wisdom is the application of the knowledge.

In the consulting business, most business owners "know" what they need to be doing. It's my job to help hold them accountable to "apply" it!

When applying your plan, here are some key elements to consider:

1. Get organized: Have a place designated to work. No distractions. Focus,especially when it comes to Internet and/or social media marketing. The Internet can be such a time-suck. You click on one link, then another, then a Facebook status. Before you know it, you've been online for 45 minutes and have not done any "work."

2. Focus: When you sit down to work, give yourself a time limit. For most strategies, 30 minutes should be plenty of time. Set a stop watch and go by it.

3. Keep a schedule: If your plan is one to twoFacebook posts per day, two blog posts per week, two email blasts to your list, etc. have it scheduled and follow it weekly. This ties back in to Commitment and Consistency in the psychology of persuasion. Remember, consistency builds trust.

4. Avoid Distractions: During your "work" time, avoid distractions like the plague. If you can get your work done in 30 minutes, do it in 30 minutes. Distractions cost you money.

5. Connect with your community: Remember that we are looking to connect and build relationships.

Listen to your community. What are their concerns? What is keeping them awake at night? What gets them excited? Listen and learn.

Then respond. This ties into your planning. Your content should always go to connect with your community.

Participate with them. People prefer to do business with people they like. Build relationships with these people.

Let's end this section with these three final thoughts:

→ Content

→ Connection

→ Community

chapter 6 | Mobile Marketing

Years ago most homes had a telephone. In the mid to late 1980s, some homes began adding another phone for their teenagers. So some homes had two phones. Fast forward until today. Many houses are now doing away with home phones altogether.

Now everyone has mobile phones with them 24 hours per day, seven days a week.

Now the demanding trend is smart phones. Companies are competing over data plans because people want Internet on their phones. And the trend is not slowing down.

Because of this, you are going to want to implement more and more mobile marketing campaigns for your company. Let's look at some different ways to use mobile phones to reach your clients.

1. Create a mobile-friendly website. Your actual website should appear different on a desktop browser compared to a mobile phone browser. A mobile browser will be very easy for your

prospect to navigate. Make sure your site is setup for mobile browsing. It is a must!

2. Text Messaging (SMS). Recently I read that almost 98% of text messages are opened. That is HUGE! Industry average open rates for emails are roughly 20%. I have seen text message marketing work unbelievably well for restaurants, churches, mechanics. It's very affordable and effective.

3. Mobile Banner Ads. This is very similar to banner ads on regular desktop websites. Another great way to grow your business.

4. Mobile emails. Depending on which email account or auto-responder service you use, they offer regular text message and html messaging. I prefer to use text message emails simply because I personally would rather read an email message in that way. You will want to keep these emails narrow also.

5. Mobile search. Google, Bing, Yahoo, etc.

6. QR Codes. These are the square black and white designs that you see on signs from time to time. You can program these to go or share just about any information. Smart phones have apps that will allow you to take a picture of these QR

codes and your phone's browser can pull up the company's website, Facebook page, etc.

7. Check-Ins. Mobile apps like Facebook, Yelp, Foursquare, Google+, just to name a few, allow their members to "checkin" on their social sites. This can be extremely beneficial to you because every check-in at your business alerts all of your clients' friends they have chosen to do business with you. Encourage your clients to "Check-In."

8. Phone Calls. What?! Believe it or not, people still talk on their phones. Call them sometimes. There are actually services available today that allow you to call a customer's cell phone and have it go automatically to their voicemail! You can broadcast a call to your database while sounding very personal, letting them know of a special promotion you are running. Very strong!

chapter 7 | How to Effectively Communicate Your Message Through Your Content.

Your goal through online and offline marketing is for these three things:

1. Getting the right people

2. In front of the right message

3. At the right time.

Earlier in the book we discussed the 5 C's of Social Media Marketing. Let's touch on those again briefly.

1. Crowd: This represents everyone online. This is not your target audience. This is too large. The good news is that somewhere within that crowd is more customers than you can ever service. Let's go find them.

2. Community: This is your ideal client. You first must get into the heads of your perfect prospect and learn how they think. The more you understand them, the more effectively you

will be able to communicate your marketing message.

3. Concerns: This goes back to your community. What keeps them awake at night? What problems do they have that you can solve?

4. Content: This will be your articles, blog posts, videos, audio interviews, etc. Your content must speak directly to your community. We will discuss this again in a minute.

5. Customer/Client. When you have properly placed quality content in front of the right people, with the right message, at the right time, you will bring in clients by the loads.

An effective formula for strong sales copy:

Problem + Aggravate + Solution = Sales

Your prospective client has a problem. Anytime you are communicating with them, whether that's developing content or other advertising mediums, you have to remind them they have a problem or a need that needs to be solved.

Your second step in that message is to aggravate that problem. Point out that if the problem is not taken care of, it will cost more to repair down the road.

Then close with your solution. Communicate that you understand exactly what they need and you can solve it for them.

Did I get "Sold" by neurosurgeon?

I was recently diagnosed with a Chiari 1 Malformation. In short, my brain was putting extra pressure on my spinal cord. After a visit to three different neurosurgeons, it was obvious surgery was needed.

After all of the imaging, testing, and consulting was done, I realized that he had used this formula on me. By no means am I saying that I did not need the surgery. He just laid it out in a way that allowed me to "accept" or "buy" it.

1. The Problem: Severe pressure on my spinal cord.

2. Aggravate: Now that I was having symptoms, he assured me they will progress. It wasn't a matter of "if" I have the surgery, it was a matter of when.

3. Solution: Surgery. We did our research and knew that he was one of the leading surgeons for this procedure. People traveled from all over the world to use him.

The point should be well-taken. Communicate your clients' problem. Let them know the problem will get worse and possibly more expensive to repair later. Then provide the solution.

5 Best Types of Content:

This can be articles, blog posts, emails, videos, audios, etc. Try to keep in mind the 80/20 rule when it comes to content. Give value; 80% of your content should be value-driven, leaving 20% available for promotion.

1. Information: This can be about your company, product, services in general. Not necessarily promotions being offered.

2. Education: Consider this the "How-To." People find great value in how-to info. Most searches online are people trying to answer something to do with "how to…" This builds trust.

3. Inspiration: Success stories of other clients are great for this type of content. It could be a testimonial directly from the client (video, letter, etc.) or it could be you sharing a recent story of success in your business. This builds Social Acceptance. Remember to always ask for referrals and testimonials.

4. Entertainment: Be real. Maybe it's someone's birthday in the office and you guys threw a surprise party. That's content. People like to do business with people they like. This lets them know you guys are real people. Just do not overdo it.

5. Promotional: This content is about anything sales-oriented: Specials, Bonuses, Coupons, etc.

Your goal in communicating with your prospect is to get them to reduce tension and increase cooperation. When you remind them of their problem, agitate that problem. That will cause tension inside of their mind. Try and think how they think. You want to present your solution in a way that you are removing that tension from their shoulders. Let them know you can and will help. This increases cooperation in their mind and speeds along the buying process.

One closing thought about effective communication with your prospects. In Stephen Covey's classic book, *7 Habits of Highly Effective People*, he covered one of the most memorable chapters of any self-help type book I have ever read. This one chapter has probably made me more money than any other chapter of a book that I can remember.

Make sure to read Habit # 5: Seek First to Understand, Then be Understood. I will leave the rest to you.

How to Use The Internet to Slash Your Advertising Budget While Getting More Leads and Customers

I know you get calls from all sorts of media outlets and organizations looking to get a piece of your advertising budget.

Today I am not pitching you anything. I would just like to tell you why businesses like yours are changing their advertising strategy. Actually, "why" they are making these changes is perfectly clear. Simply put, the return on investment is much higher.

More customers. More leads. For less cost.

Google's mission has provided the opportunity for every type of businesses to flourish in ways that were impossible before.

When people want to find something, buy something, research a purchase, they jump on the Internet – at home or on their phone and do a search. If they don't see your business in the results, they won't know you exist; won't buy from you. It's that simple.

Whatever you are paying for newspaper, radio or other such traditional advertising – your dollars will go much further online. However, getting online traffic into your business can be very confusing.

Web designers will say you need a new website.

Search engine optimization experts will argue that the problem lies in your low ranking.

Copywriters will say that it's your marketing message.

Social networking experts will say you need to be Tweeting, and Facebooking, etc.

Yellow Pages reps will say you *must have* an ad in the Online Yellow Pages.

Branding experts will say, yes, you guessed it, the branding and positioning of your company is the problem.

And then there are the larger advertising agencies that take care of all of the above. They'll say *everything* is the problem.

I wonder. Who is really on your side? Who is looking at the big picture?

Unlike any other type of traditional advertising (newspaper, magazines, radio, tv),...

→ Internet marketing can be tracked for results: number of searches, clicks, page views etc. So, you'll know right away whether your online presence is bringing in business.

→ Search engine rankings are self-evident. Higher rankings = more traffic coming into your business than lower rankings (your competitors).

→ Internet marketing can be optimized over time to ratchet up traffic coming into the business. With analytics installed, it's easy to see where the weak links are and optimize them for ever more traffic and conversion.

There's nothing pie-in-the-sky about marketing online. It's safe, trackable and is by far the highest return on investment compared to any other advertising outlet.

I understand that what you really need is someone to take care of your online marketing that you can trust. The first step you'll want to take is for that person to show you exactly where you rank online and where your competitors rank. This data is freely available to anyone with an Internet connection. If you like, I can give you this data free of charge.

Now, let's dig a little deeper...

The Big Advertising Shift

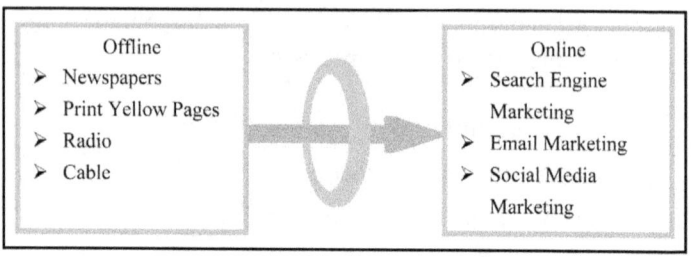

Consider the following consumer behavior:

→ "70% of US household now use the Internet as an information source when shopping locally for products and services" (Kelsey Group)

→ 31% of all <u>business buyers</u> turn to a Search Engine first when looking for a locally based product or service

→ Product Research and Comparison shopping happens online, but 67% of those purchases happen *offline(Accenture)*

→ 90% of purchases are made within 50 miles of a person's home *(Kelsey)*

Consider the following local search data:

→ 43% of all searches on the Google network included a geographical identifier.

   * 86% of those people followed up with a phone call

   * 61% of those people ended up making a purchase offline

→ 25% of all commercial Internet Searches are conducted by users looking for Local Merchants *(Kelsey)*

→ 35% of all Searches are 'local' *(DM News)*

→ 84% of U.S. based Internet users performed local searches, or 129 million people, and were looking for a local business

→ Advertising spent for local search

   * $3 Billion in 2008 (*Kelsey)*

   * $13 Billion by 2010 *(Forbes)*

Search Engines drive more traffic to a website than ALL other mediums combined!

The point is local businesses are transferring their spending from traditional means to an online medium.

A fresh and focused approach.

You may have tried some online marketing tactics in the past and failed. You're the norm, not the exception.

Online marketing is easy, just not simple to learn. There is just so much bad information out there.

Incapable people are slamming the industry, and failures are giving the industry a bad name.

Be very careful of those things people tell you that they 'tweaked' a website to rank higher. Here is a document (website) put together by Google that EVERY buyer of online services needs to see.

http://is.gd/41j8e

(paste this into your browser and you'll be sent to a Google page)

Here are a few things from Google's site:

→ **Be wary of SEO firms and web consultants or agencies that send you email out of the blue.**

→ **No one can guarantee a #1 ranking on Google**

→ **Be careful if a company is secretive or won't clearly explain what they intend to do**

→ **Be sure to understand where the money goes**

Websites

Do you remember when people would visit a family doctor if anything was wrong?

That doctor was essentially a jack-of-all-trades in the medical field. Their advice was the end all, be all.

Now medicine has sub-sectors. Doctors specialize into neurology and other medical fields. In fact, there are subspecialties of the neurology specialty.

There is a specialist for everything.

Way, way back in 1995 there was the IT guy. He knew IT, software and websites.

He was so smart, everyone looked up to him. Now days I still get called an IT geek, but that is dead wrong.

Just because I work on the Internet, I should know how to fix the computer?

Sure, I probably know more than most, but don't call me to fix your computer.

You wouldn't hire a carpenter to sell your house. Don't hire a web developer to market your website.

Make sure you understand that marketing a website is completely different from creating a website.

Imagine a site that doesn't speak to the right audience.

Imagine if you could just double the call-to-action rates (call you, email you, fill out a form, etc.) on the site with a small investment.

Simple keyword research will demonstrate that people are looking for product or service – in your area - right now!

Once you have that traffic streaming to your site, you must maximize the conversion and the website is a critical component.

A website should touch five separate hands:

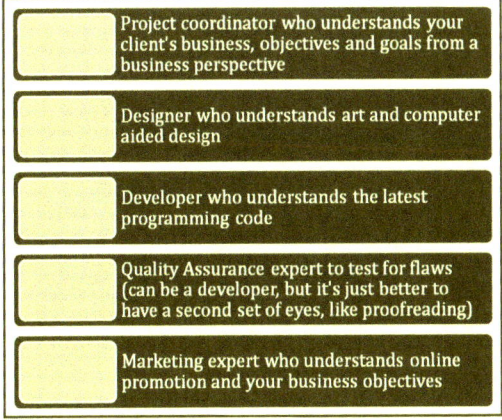

White and Black Hat Online Marketing

In the days of old western movies, the good guys wore the white hats and the bad guys wore the black hats.

This is no different in our current world of online marketing.

We have all heard of spam email. Something that is spam comes from someone who is black hat.

Another example of black hat online marketing is using techniques that are disapproved of by the search engines in order to increase your rankings.

Basically, you're trying to fool the search engines.

White hat is where we play.

This is the more difficult route to win online in the short-term; however, it is the most sustainable and ultimately conforms to the guidelines set forth by the online community who represent paying customers to any local business.

Don't try and fool the search engines!

Since it all comes down to the search engines, you must understand their role.

A search engine's job is to provide the most relevant results to a web surfer for the search query requested. Period.

Back in 1998 when Google was founded they gained tremendous market share for one main reason.

It wasn't their marketing. It was their algorithm.

An algorithm is a mathematical function (equation) the search engines use to determine the ranking of a webpage (notice I said webpage, not website!).

Google's algorithm is so good that by 2002 both MSN (now Bing) and Yahoo! had followed Google's style of ranking.

Since the search engines' role is to provide relevant results, the way they determine if a webpage is relevant is very important.

But their algorithm is constantly changing, thereby making it very difficult to completely understand what is needed to rank in the top spots.

I don't like this cat and mouse game.

I'd rather be proactive rather than reactive.

It's about quality efforts, folks!

Quality of inbound links, *not* quantity. Quality of social sites you're on, *not* volume. Quality of your web pages, *not* quantity of pages.

I don't expect this to change or ever go obsolete.

We may add a new strategy, or change a couple of our processes or measurements, but for the most part, the system will remain the same.

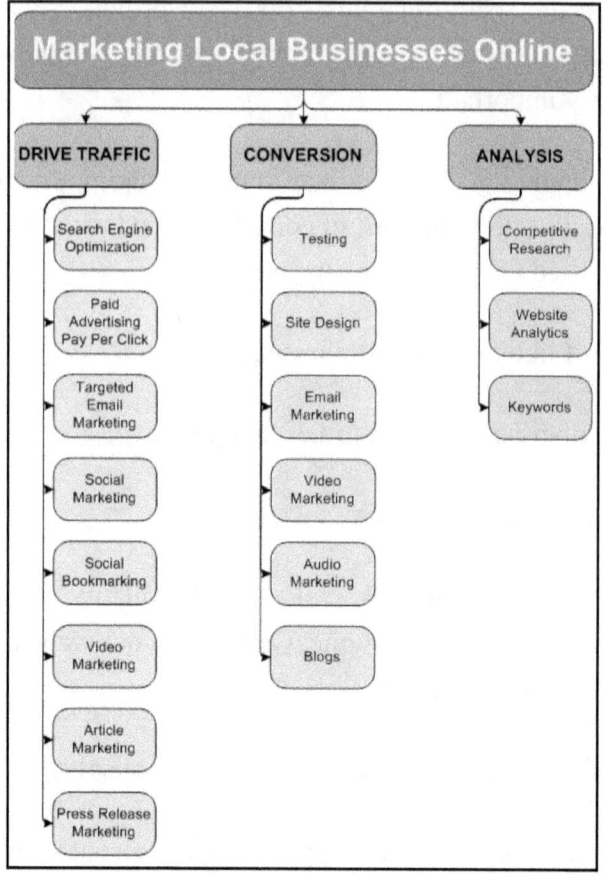

Marketing Toolbox

You have probably been in business for several years marketing yourself to the local community through traditional means such as word of mouth, radio, television, newspapers, yellow pages, conventions, trade shows and charity events, among many others.

While taking an offline business online is exciting, there are many, many ways you can spin your tires and never gain any traction.

There are many ways to spend time and money in areas that simply don't work.

Marketing online is merely positioning your website in front of those people when they are researching a specific service or product and compelling them to action.

Marketing Assessment

Our no cost website assessment is a not a sales pitch. We know exactly why you're website is not performing and we'll tell you.

We'll tell you how many people are searching for your product or service on Google.

We'll tell you how strong the competition is. We'll even give you some reports that you can keep.

We promise we'll never put pressure to buy our services, that goes against all of our philosophies. It's simple, that if you ever purchase online marketing services, we want the chance to earn the right to your business.

Call us at 409-291-4030 to book an assessment
Or
Visit us online at BeaumontSocialMedia.com